ABOUT THE BOOK

How many bones do you have? What are bones made of? How do they grow? If you break a bone, how does it heal? How do bones help you hear? These and many other questions about bones are answered in this book, the latest in a series by Edith Weart about the fascinating way your body functions. The author describes how bones and muscles work together, how bones protect the vital organs of your body — your heart and brain. A final chapter tells how archaeologists have learned from "dead" bones about the daily life of prehistoric man. From the way a bone has been broken they can even detect murders committed thousands of years ago.

A simple, lucid text, accurate information, and attractive three-color illustrations add up to an exciting and authoritative book.

You can learn more about how your body works in these other books by Edith Lucie Weart.

THE STORY OF YOUR BONES

1 Bones of cranium
2 Bones of the face
3 Bones of the ear
4 Hyoid bone in neck
5 Cervical vertebrae
6 Thoracic vertebrae
7 Lumbar vertebrae
8 Sacral vertebrae
9 Coccygeal vertebrae
10 The twenty-four ribs
11 Sternum protects heart
12 Clavical
13 Scapula (shoulder blade)
14 Humerus in upper arm
15 Ulna in lower arm
16 Radius in lower arm
17 Carpus in wrist
18 Metacarpals in hand
19 Phalanges in fingers
20 Hipbones
21 Femur (thighbone)
22 Patella (kneecap)
23 Tibia (shinbone)
24 Fibula in lower leg
25 Tarsus
26 Metatarsus in foot
27 Phalanges in toes

The Story of Your Bones

by Edith Lucie Weart
illustrated by Jan Fairservis

Coward-McCann, Inc.
New York

Because she is an unusually nice sister-in-law
this book is dedicated to
Janet

092013

Library of Congress Catalog Card Number: AC 66-10208

PRINTED IN THE UNITED STATES OF AMERICA

Contents

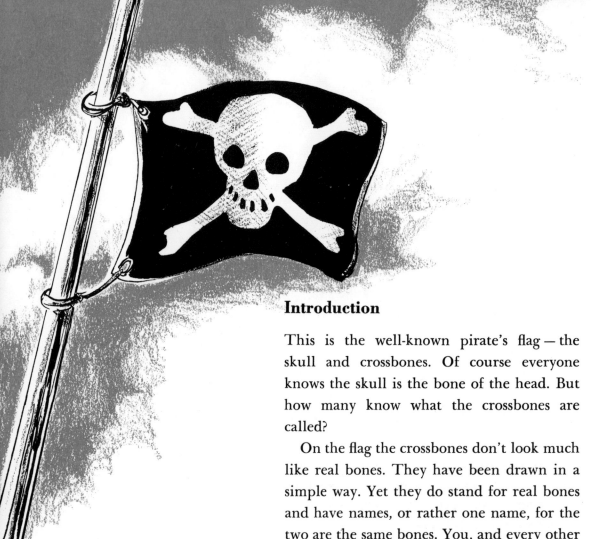

Introduction

This is the well-known pirate's flag — the skull and crossbones. Of course everyone knows the skull is the bone of the head. But how many know what the crossbones are called?

On the flag the crossbones don't look much like real bones. They have been drawn in a simple way. Yet they do stand for real bones and have names, or rather one name, for the two are the same bones. You, and every other human, have two of them — the heaviest and longest bones in the body. If you feel your own bones you can make a good guess which are the crossbones.

8

They are the bones in the upper part of the legs — the thighbones. The thighbone has a scientific name; it is called the femur (fee'-mur).

There are many bones in your body and each has a name. For example, the skull is sometimes called the cranium (kray'-nee-um). Actually it isn't just one bone, but a number of bones joined together.

The bones of the pirate's flag, then, could be called the cranium and femora. (Femora is the plural of femur.) However, skull and crossbones is certainly an easier way to describe it.

It is uncertain when and why pirates adopted this flag.

However, this is not a book about pirates or their flag. It is a book about bones, human bones, your bones.

How many bones are there in the human body? What are bones made of? Do they grow, and how? If a bone is broken how does it mend?

This book answers all these questions, and tells a lot more about bones, too.

A Baby Has More Bones Than Its Father or Mother

When a baby is born he has 270 growth centers of bone. His father or mother has only 206 separate bones. Why is this?

Of course it is plain to see that babies grow. As they grow, new bones are formed. An example is the bones of the wrist, which are called carpals (kar'-pals). When a baby is born he has no bones in his wrist at all.

Age	Number of carpals
2 years	2
3 years	3
5 years	5
6 years	6
8 years	7
12 years	8

And so it is in the ankle and in certain other parts of the body.

The question then is this: What happens during the growing-up period while a boy becomes a man and a girl a woman?

As a child begins to be grown-up some of his bones become "fused." They grow together to form one bone from two or more. A child has 33 bones in his backbone, bones called vertebrae (vert'-eh-bray). But the sacral vertebrae, which are five, fuse to become one, and make up the sacrum (say'-krum) — the large bone at the bottom of the back on which the backbone rests. Below the sacral vertebrae a child has four more bones,

CARPALS

These are girls' hands. Girls develop carpals earlier than boys. Growth is not complete until a boy or girl is about 18 years old.

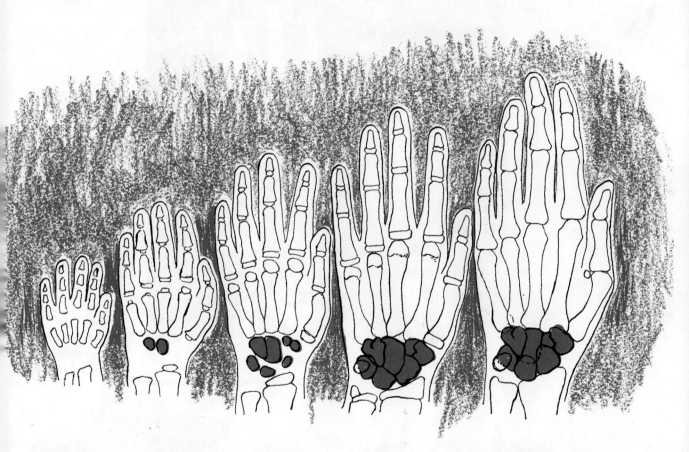

Infant   2 years   6 years   12 years   18 years

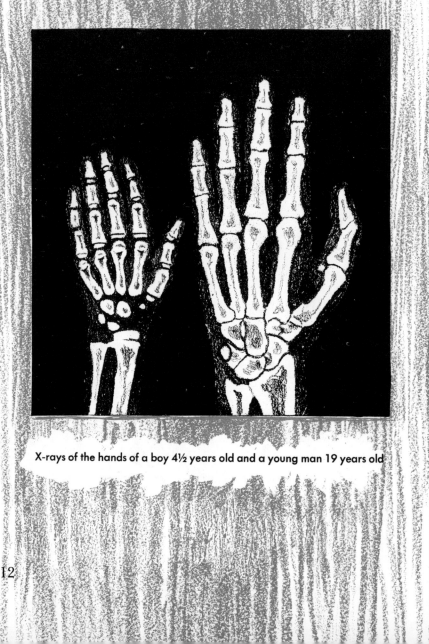

X-rays of the hands of a boy 4½ years old and a young man 19 years old

but in the grown-up these fuse to become one, called the coccyx (kok'-siks).

These are just some examples of what happens in the growing-up period. Of course you may grow at a different rate than one of your friends, or than your sister or brother. However, the growth of the bones is so nearly exact that it is possible to tell a normal child's age quite accurately just by looking at an x-ray of his hand.

If you are interested in the names of the 206 bones which a grown-up has you will find them listed on pages 14-16. When you look at this list you will find that there are two of some bones, such as the femur, the thighbone. A man (and a woman too, of course) has two legs, therefore there is a femur in the right leg and one in the left leg. And so it is with other bones of the legs, and the bones of the arms, of the hands, and feet, and other paired parts of the body.

A good many of these bones can be easily felt. Start at the head. It is impossible to tell the different parts of the skull from each other. They fit too closely together. They have to, in order to protect the brain which is inside them. But the lower jaw — the mandible (man'-deh-bl) — can be felt without any trouble at all.

It is also easy to feel the sternum (stur'-num), the breastbone. It is certainly possible to count the ribs. On a thin person they can actually be seen. You might look at the picture of the skeleton on pages 15-16 and see how many of these bones you can feel in your own body.

APPROXIMATE NUMBER OF BONES OF THE ADULT HUMAN BODY (206)

THE HEAD

cranium

occipital	1
parietal	2
frontal	1
temporal	2
sphenoid	1
ethmoid	1
	8

face

nasal	2
vomer	1
inferior nasal concha	2
lacrimal	2
zygomatic (maler)	2
palatine (palate)	2
maxilla	2
mandible	1
	14

ear

malleus	2
incus	2
stapes	2
	6

hyoid

bone in neck	1

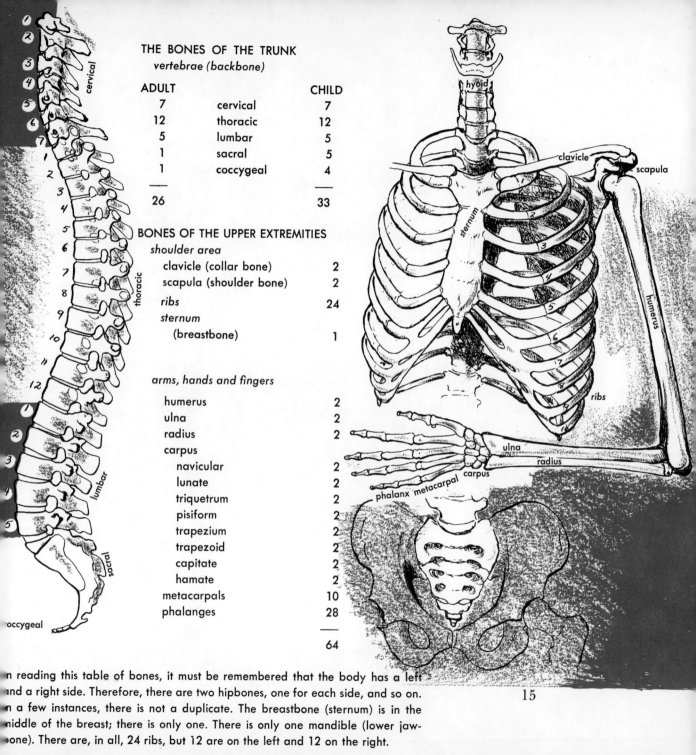

THE BONES OF THE TRUNK
vertebrae (backbone)

ADULT		CHILD
7	cervical	7
12	thoracic	12
5	lumbar	5
1	sacral	5
1	coccygeal	4
26		33

BONES OF THE UPPER EXTREMITIES

shoulder area	
clavicle (collar bone)	2
scapula (shoulder bone)	2
ribs	24
sternum	
(breastbone)	1
arms, hands and fingers	
humerus	2
ulna	2
radius	2
carpus	
navicular	2
lunate	2
triquetrum	2
pisiform	2
trapezium	2
trapezoid	2
capitate	2
hamate	2
metacarpals	10
phalanges	28
	64

In reading this table of bones, it must be remembered that the body has a left and a right side. Therefore, there are two hipbones, one for each side, and so on. In a few instances, there is not a duplicate. The breastbone (sternum) is in the middle of the breast; there is only one. There is only one mandible (lower jaw-bone). There are, in all, 24 ribs, but 12 are on the left and 12 on the right.

15

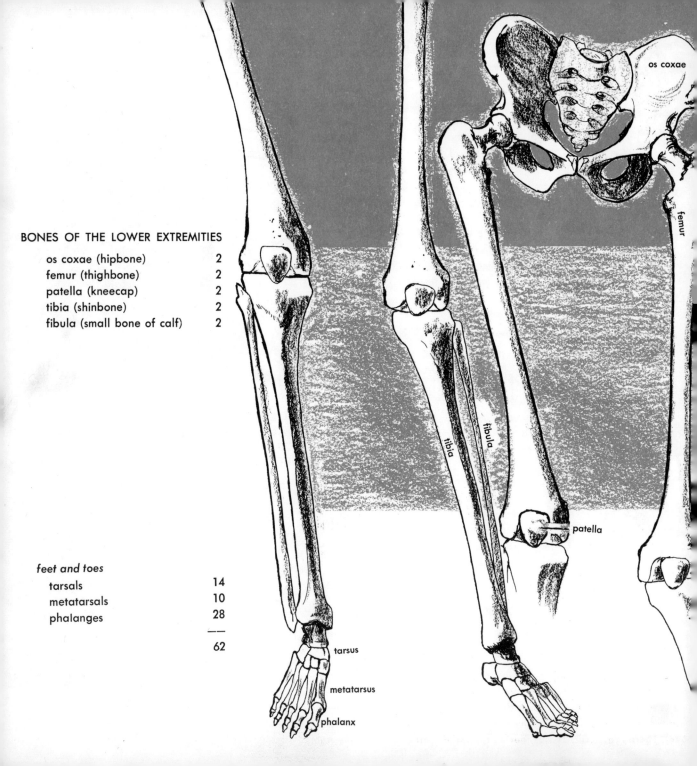

BONES OF THE LOWER EXTREMITIES

os coxae (hipbone)	2
femur (thighbone)	2
patella (kneecap)	2
tibia (shinbone)	2
fibula (small bone of calf)	2

feet and toes

tarsals	14
metatarsals	10
phalanges	28
	——
	62

os coxae

os coxae

femur

femur

fibula

tibia

patella

tarsus

metatarsus

phalanx

Age Makes a Difference in the
Size and Shape of Bones

Have you ever noticed the differences between a baby's head and that of its grandfather or grandmother? Between the baby's head and its mother's? Take a look sometime. The baby's head is very round and seems large for such a small body.

You may also have noticed that there are soft spots on a baby's head. The skull is not hard everywhere as yours is. Such a soft spot is called a fontanel (fon'-tah-nel). The fontanels are spaces between bones of the skull which allow room for the bones to grow. There are six fontanels, but only two can be felt as soft spots on the infant's head. The one at the back of the head will disappear when the baby is about two months old, but the one at the front won't close until the child is a year or a year and a half old. The bones of the skull will then have grown until they fit tightly together.

Not only is a baby's head bigger in comparison with its body than the head of an adult is, but the shape is different, too. You can see the differences in the pictures on the next page.

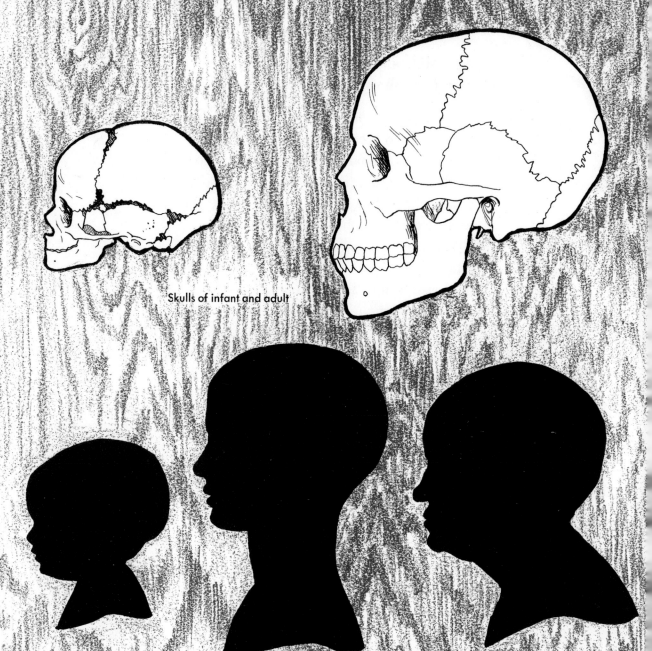

Skulls of infant and adult

18

Profiles of infant, adult, and older person

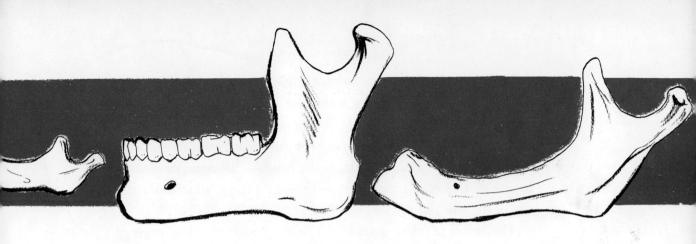

Mandibles of infant, adult, and older person

There is a great difference in the shape of the mandible (lower jawbone) at various ages, which in part makes a baby's face so unlike that of his grandparents. At birth the lower jaw is little more than a shell with a few sockets for teeth. At four years of age the shape is quite changed. All the "milk" or temporary teeth are now in place in the upper and lower jaw. After the milk teeth are lost and the permanent teeth come in, the jaw is much bigger. It has to be because the permanent teeth are much larger than the milk teeth and there are more of them. There are 20 milk teeth and 32 permanent teeth.

As people get very old they usually lose most of their teeth. Not many people of seventy or older have more than a few of their own teeth left. When the teeth are lost the jawbone shrinks. This changes the whole shape of the face. This picture shows these changes in the mandible.

Of course other bones change too. How else could a baby only a couple of feet long (or less) become a man six feet tall?

The skull doesn't grow as much as other parts of the body, for it is already quite large when the baby is born. The adult head is only twice the size of the newborn infant's head. Most of the growth takes place during the first five years. At the end of this time the circumference of the head — the measure around it — is 20 inches. At twelve years it is 21 inches, practically the size of the adult head.

The bones of other parts of the body grow more. The arms of the adult are four times as long as those of the baby; the legs five times as long. Measure your legs and a baby's legs to see the difference. Of course arms and legs are just examples. All bones grow.

There are differences between boys and girls, too. Not so much when they are small, but when they get to be about fourteen or so, as they begin to change into men and women. You can see this for yourself. Young men have broad shoulders and are small around the hips; just the opposite is true of women.

Women look larger around the hips because they *are* larger. It isn't because they are fat. A woman's pelvis is a different shape from a man's. Even in the newborn infant there is a difference between the pelvis of a boy and that of a girl. The lower part of the trunk of the body is called the pelvis. Pelvis (pel'-vis) is a Latin word meaning basin, and this is, indeed, its shape. The pelvis helps to protect the organs in the lower part of the abdomen. It is made up of the right and left os coxae (hipbones) which connect at the front. In back they join the sacrum and coccyx. The pelvis supports the spine and in turn rests on the upper part of the legs. You have already read that the sacrum in the child is made up of 5 bones and the coccyx of 4, but in the grown-up the sacrum is just one bone and so is the coccyx. So with the hipbones: what were three bones is now one. They fuse when the child is about fifteen years old. The 5 bones of the sacrum do not become united until about the age of twenty.

The pelvis of a man is narrow. A woman's pelvis is wide and broad, to give room for an infant being born to pass through the birth canal.

Of course there are differences between boys and between girls, too. Some are short, some are tall, even though they are the same age. You may be taller — or shorter — than your best friend, even though you are same age. Some of this depends on the rate at which you are growing, for growing is sometimes done in spurts. You may be taller now, but your friend may catch up with you in a couple of years.

21

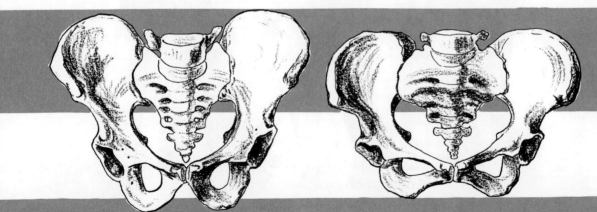

Male pelvis   Female pelvis

Then too, heredity plays a part. If your parents are short, you may be short. If they are tall, you will probably be tall. If your mother is short and your father very tall, when you are grown you will probably be taller than your mother but shorter than your father. However, there is nothing sure about it.

How do bones grow? You will read about this farther on in this book. But first let's find out what bones are made of.

What Bones Are and How They Grow

Have you ever seen a human bone? Unless you have seen a skeleton in a doctor's office, or in a museum of natural history, you probably haven't. There aren't many people who have seen a human bone.

You have, however, seen a great many animal bones — and so has everyone else. A lamb chop contains part of a rib and a vertebra; a leg of lamb is a thighbone or femur; spareribs of pork are, as the name tells you, ribs of a pig — the long part of the rib, not the part that is attached to a vertebra, as the bone of a lamb chop is. A veal cutlet has a round bone in it — this is bone from the lower leg of a calf. You can learn a lot about the shape of bones by visiting a butcher's shop, or even by looking at the bones in the meat you eat. Remember, there is a difference in size and shape between the bones in your body and the bones in an animal.

What are bones made of? Rock? Cement?

Not at all. When the animal is alive its bones are alive, too. Bones are living tissue, called osseous (os'-e-us) tissue from the Latin word for bone which is os. Yet it is true that in some ways bone tissue does resemble rock. Like rock it contains minerals, some of which are the same as the minerals in rock. However, bone is unlike rock because it is not solid mineral.

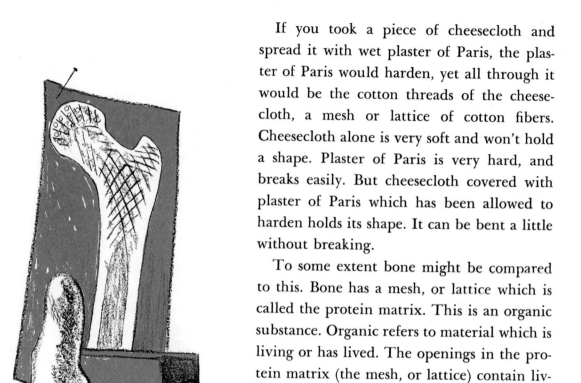

If you took a piece of cheesecloth and spread it with wet plaster of Paris, the plaster of Paris would harden, yet all through it would be the cotton threads of the cheesecloth, a mesh or lattice of cotton fibers. Cheesecloth alone is very soft and won't hold a shape. Plaster of Paris is very hard, and breaks easily. But cheesecloth covered with plaster of Paris which has been allowed to harden holds its shape. It can be bent a little without breaking.

To some extent bone might be compared to this. Bone has a mesh, or lattice which is called the protein matrix. This is an organic substance. Organic refers to material which is living or has lived. The openings in the protein matrix (the mesh, or lattice) contain living bone cells of different shapes and sizes, but chiefly the space is filled with inorganic material, very, very tiny crystals of minerals, chiefly of different compounds of calcium, such as calcium phosphate.

It is possible to prove that bone is made of

two different kinds of material — organic (proteinlike matrix) and inorganic (minerals). Take the bone of a lamb chop. Carefully scrape off all the meat and fat. Place the cleaned bone in a jar of weak acid. Ordinary vinegar will do. Cover the jar. Every couple of days pour out the old vinegar and add new. Otherwise forget about it for a few weeks. At the end of this time you will find that the vinegar has dissolved out all the mineral, the inorganic material. Only the protein matrix of the bone is left, the organic material. This matrix will have the size and shape of the bone with which you started the experiment. It will be very flexible indeed because the minerals will be dissolved out.

If you use a longer rib bone, perhaps a sparerib, and dissolve out all the minerals with vinegar, you can bend it without breaking it. Perhaps it will be possible to tie a knot in it, if the bone is long enough.

If a bone is burned — not an easy thing to do in a house or apartment — the protein matrix will be dissolved and only the minerals will remain as a model of the original bone. This model is very brittle. It breaks easily.

How hard or how stiff the bone is depends on the proportion of inorganic to organic material in it. If it were all inorganic, that is made up entirely of minerals, it would be very hard but very brittle, and would break easily. If, on the other hand, it were made up entirely of organic material, it wouldn't be stiff enough to hold its shape, and would bend much too easily.

This is what bony tissue, osseous tissue, is like — a tissue made up of minerals and a protein matrix. But a bone, as most of us think of it, is more than this. Bones contain hollow spaces filled with a soft substance called marrow. There are two kinds of marrow: red marrow and yellow marrow. Yellow marrow is found chiefly in the middle part of the cavities of the long bones. It has many fat cells. Red marrow is found in the cavities at the ends of the long bones and in the flat bones such as the sternum (breastbone) and ribs. It is in the red marrow that the red blood cells and most of the white blood cells are made. These blood cells pass out of the bones into the blood itself.

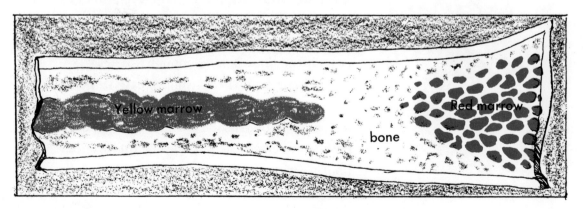

Yellow marrow   bone   Red marrow

Bone is osseous tissue

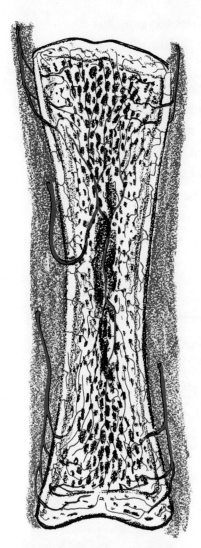

Blood vessels run through
canals in the bones.

Bone tissue has both arteries and veins, some small and some large. Though it looks very dense, even under a microscope, there really are many open spaces in it. Tiny canals run through the bones. The blood vessels enter the bone through these canals.

Arteries are the very large blood vessels which carry blood from the heart; veins are those which carry it back again. Arteries divide into smaller and smaller blood vessels until they are so small that only a single blood cell can pass through them. These tiny blood vessels are called capillaries and are the link between the arteries and veins. At their other end they join with very tiny veins, which in turn join larger veins, until there is just one big vein leading into the heart. As the blood is carried around the body it reaches the cells in the lungs. There it takes up oxygen from the air in the lungs. This oxygen is bound to the red part of the red blood cell which is called hemoglobin. As the capillaries touch the other cells in the body, the cells take up the oxygen. They use it to make the materials they need, and they give up carbon dioxide, which is a waste product. The blood in the

27

veins now carries more carbon dioxide than it does oxygen, but when it gets back to the lungs it gets rid of the carbon dioxide and takes up more oxygen.

The blood carries other substances which the body needs, such as calcium. You will read about this a few pages farther on.

Although osseous tissue, bony tissue, makes up most of the bone, it is not all alike. There are two different kinds. One is hard and there are no spaces in it. This type of bone tissue is called compact bone, a very good name for it. The other type of bone tissue, which is spongy, is called spongy or cancellous bone. It may be fine or coarse. Cancellous (kan'-se-lus) comes from a Latin word meaning lattice or framework.

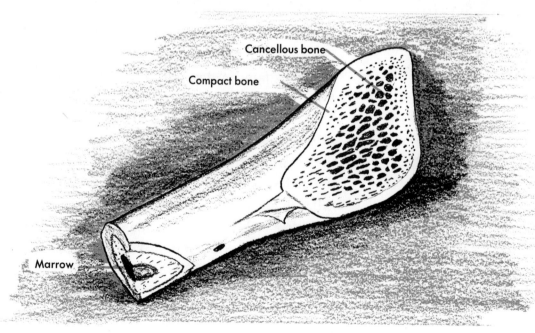

Bones contain both kinds of tissue, compact and cancellous, but how much of each kind any single bone contains depends on what bone it is.

In a long bone, such as the femur of the leg, or for that matter any bone of the arm or leg, compact bone makes up most of the long part of the bone, but the ends are made of spongy bone with just a covering of compact bone.

The round bone in a veal cutlet shows plainly the two kinds of bone tissue — for it is easy to see that the inside (next to the soft marrow in the center) is different from the outside.

The end of a long bone is called the epiphysis (e-pif'-i-sis). While the bone is growing, the epiphysis remains separated from the end of the bone itself for a long time. In fact, at first it is not bone at all, but cartilage. (In meat you would call cartilage "gristle.") Gradually, however, a change takes place in the cartilage. A center of bone appears, which becomes larger. For a long time, however, a layer of cartilage separates the epiphysis from the rest of the bone. This makes it possible for the bone to grow longer. When growth

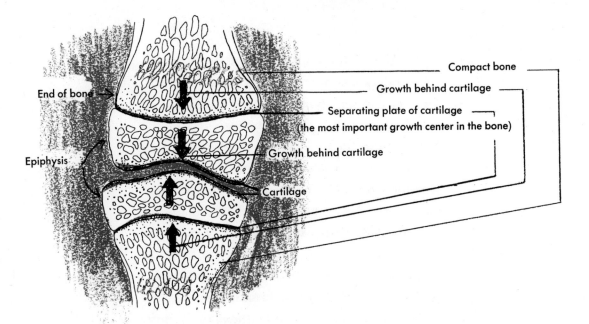

End of bone →

Epiphysis

Compact bone

Growth behind cartilage

Separating plate of cartilage
(the most important growth center in the bone)

Growth behind cartilage

Cartilage

is finished there is no separation between the long bone and the epiphysis. This is the final shape of the bone. In the case of the humerus (the largest bone of the arm) this does not happen until a boy is about twenty, although in girls it occurs about two years earlier. The same ages see the end of the growth of the femur.

In this way bones become longer. However, bones become thicker, too. More layers of bone are added on the outside. It might be compared to the way a tree grows; it is the outer layer of the tree which grows — adding layer after layer of wood. Not that the comparison is too good a one, for bone is hollow.

Bone is covered by a thin layer of membrane called the periosteum (per′-e-os′-tee-um). New bone is formed by the deepest part of the periosteum.

30

So much for the general makeup of a bone — compact bone, cancellous bone, marrow. What of the minerals in the bone?

The minerals of bones somewhat resemble the minerals of rock. Chiefly bones are made up of calcium and phosphorus, but other chemicals may also be present in small amounts. However, calcium makes up about half the weight of dry bone. The entire body of a 150-pound man is estimated to contain something like two and one-half pounds of calcium. Practically all of this, from 97 per-cent to 99 percent, is in the bones. Calcium is present largely as calcium phosphate, which, with other minerals, forms a very complex crystal. This is attached to the pro-tein matrix. Just how this is done is by no means yet certain. There is a lot about the human body that is unknown.

The minerals, in whatever way they are bound together, are present in the bone as very, very small crystals, far too small to be seen with the naked eye. The surface of the crystal is very large in proportion to its thick-ness. The surface area of all the bone crys-tals in the skeleton of a grown man is said to be more than 100 acres. One acre is 43,560 square feet, so 100 acres is a very large area indeed. This measurement is not for a large man, but for a man weighing only 154 pounds.

The materials of the bones are constantly being dissolved and carried away by the blood. At the same time the blood carries material from the food we eat to replace the bone which has been taken away. Bone changes, yet it always looks the same.

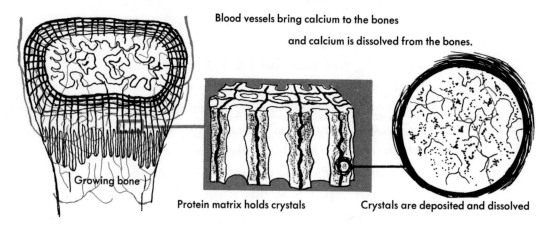

Blood vessels bring calcium to the bones and calcium is dissolved from the bones.

Growing bone

Protein matrix holds crystals

Crystals are deposited and dissolved

The exchange of minerals is especially important in the case of calcium, for too little or too much calcium in the blood can cause serious sickness. Fortunately there is a constant passage of calcium from the blood to the bone and from the bone to the blood. This goes on continuously hour-by-hour and day-by-day, so there are no sudden changes in the body. It has been thought that the entire calcium in the bones is "turned over" in about 200 days but new research indicates that it may take much longer than this.

32

To build bones both calcium and phosphorus are needed. Milk is a good supply of both. But for calcium to be absorbed from the intestines and used by the bone it is necessary to have vitamin D. This can readily be obtained by taking cod-liver oil, or by drinking vitamin D milk, which is usually easy to buy in the United States. Sunshine makes vitamin D by acting on the skin, but sunshine is not very dependable during the winter months, especially in the northern states. It is only while the bones are growing that the need for calcium, phosphorus and vitamin D is so great. Grown-ups can usually get along very well with small amounts.

It is not yet known exactly how vitamin D acts. As in so many things about the body, there is much to be learned.

Bone is very hard. It is one of the hardest structures in the body. Some bones are harder than others, however.

Although a rib breaks rather readily, for it is small, a leg is a different matter. The leg withstands pressure very well. It. is largely made up of hard compact bone. When you jump down from a high place, you put a lot of pressure on your legs, but they can take it.

Some of the credit for this must be given to the feet. The foot is remarkably well built to withstand pressure. The arch of the foot has just the shape which is best for this. Then too, the weight is put on a foot, by jumping, or just walking, the toes spread out so that all the weight does not come on one spot. One-fourth of the weight is borne by the big toe, one-fourth by the other toes, and the remaining one-half by the heel. Just consider — the feet can hold up under the weight of even the largest man.

The pressure which the body exerts can be fantastic. This was plain to see when women started wearing spike-heeled shoes. The heels have rods of steel inside them, and

Bones of the foot

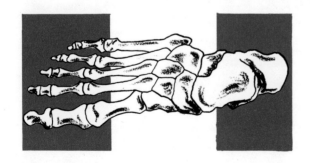 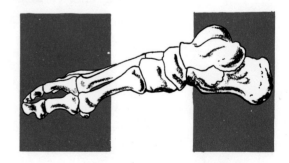

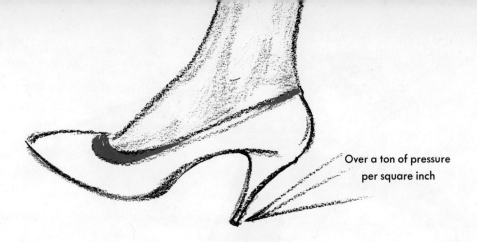

Over a ton of pressure
per square inch

the bottoms are very small. All the weight of the body rests on the feet — half of it on the heels. In walking one heel comes down first, so all the weight of the body is on that small heel for a moment. And of course the heel isn't put down softly, but with a lot of energy. Spike heels can make dents in very, very hard floors, yet the bone of the heel and the leg are not hurt.

I suppose every boy and girl has, at some time, broken an arm or a leg or knows someone who has had a broken bone. The doctor put on a plaster cast and after a number of weeks, or possibly months, the arm or leg was as good is new. The bone had healed.

Except to keep the bone that was broken from moving, probably nothing was done. The bone healed itself. How was this possible? Turn to the next page to read about it.

Broken Bones Made As Good As New

It isn't really very easy to break a bone. Think of the many times you have slid on the ice and fallen or jumped from a high spot, lost your balance and landed on knees or arms. Your skin has been scraped; you have been black and blue. Broken bones? No.

Yet now and then a bone does break in an accident. If you break an arm, for instance, you can't use it. It may have a funny shape; part may go off at a slight angle, or there may be a bump in it. And it hurts, how it hurts!

Sometimes children's bones may be bent out of shape, rather than broken into two or more parts. Young bones have more organic material than adult bones. They are, therefore, more flexible. They bend easily, something like a stick of green wood. For this

36

reason such an injury is called a greenstick fracture. The bones of old people are much more brittle and break more easily than the bones of a child.

The doctor probably takes an x-ray picture of the arm, or whatever part of the body has been hurt. The x-ray will show how the fragments of the bone are placed, whether they are widely apart, off at an angle, or close together. Once he knows this he can put the broken parts in place again. This is called "reducing the fracture." The patient is usually given something so that he will not feel pain while this is being done.

After the fracture is reduced the broken bone must be kept from moving until it has a chance to heal. In the case of an arm or leg

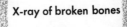

X-ray of broken bones

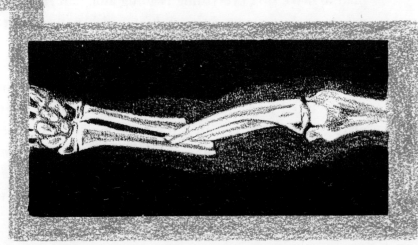

the limb is usually surrounded with plaster of Paris — a cast. In the case of bones of other parts of the body it may be sufficient simply to hold them in place by strapping the skin over the broken bone with adhesive tape. The important thing is to keep the broken bone from moving.

After this, the doctor does very little except to check now and then to make sure everything is going along all right. It is up to nature to do the rest. It is a job at which nature is very good, indeed.

From the moment the bone is broken, your body goes to work to repair the damage. Broken blood vessels in the bone and muscle bleed into the tissue. Blood flows into all parts of the place of the fracture — into the bone marrow, the bone covering (the periosteum), the canals of the bone. The first step in healing is the clotting of this blood, which takes place in only a few minutes. This is an early bridging of the gap between the fragments of the bone, a framework for the cells which will form new bone and eventually heal the fracture. In young people new bone begins to form within 48 hours of the accident.

Bone-forming cells located in the covering and lining of the bone become very active at the place where the bone is broken. They send out a large amount of protein matrix and other materials to bridge the gap between the fragments of bone. This is

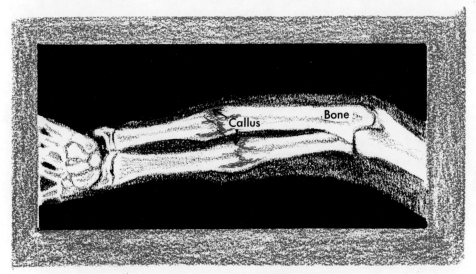

called callus. It is a new growth which has its own system of blood vessels. Gradually it hardens as new cells and minerals are deposited in the callus. After the parts of the bone are united the appearance of the callus changes and gradually the excess bone and the blood vessels all disappear. The bone begins to look normal.

New bone grows into the callus from each side of the break.

Gradually the two new bone growths meet and the gap is closed.

How long this takes depends entirely on the bone and the type of injury. Each bone in the body has its own healing time. The bones of the arms heal faster than those of the legs. It may take as long as six months or more for the tibia and femur to heal. Of course these bones have to bear the weight of the body. If the ends of the two parts of the broken bone touch each other — as they should if reduced properly — they may heal in a couple of months. In a young child it may take only three weeks. Fractures where the fragments of bone are widely apart take much longer to unite and in very rare cases may not unite at all.

Children produce more callus than older people. This may be the reason their fractures heal faster. It is important that the bone be without any movement during the healing process. If it isn't it may not heal at all.

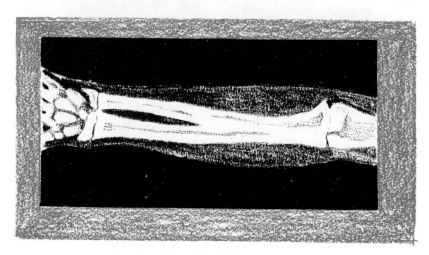

X-ray of healed fractures

Three Very Special Bones Which Help You Hear

You can see your ear in a mirror. You can feel it. Do you know the name of the bone just under the ear? Do you know the bones inside this bone and how they help you hear?

The bone you can feel under the ear is the temporal (tem'-po-ral) bone. Within it lie many canals which connect the *outer ear* (the one you can see and feel) with the *middle ear,* a small cavity filled with air inside the temporal bone. Between the two is the tympanic (tim-pan'-ik) membrane, which is commonly called the eardrum. The middle ear connects with the *inner ear* by a very small opening. The inner ear is made up of many cavities and canals inside the temporal bone, and has in it the auditory nerve which leads sound impulses to the brain where they are interrupted into different sounds as we know them.

Inside the middle ear there are tiny bones which are important in carrying sound waves to the inner ear. The middle ear is very small. It would hold no more than five or six drops of water. If you measure this amount in a glass, you will see just how small the middle ear is, and how small the three bones in it must be.

These bones are called the malleus (mal'-e-us), incus (ing'-kus), and stapes (stay'-pees). They were given these names because someone with imagination thought they looked like a hammer, anvil, and stirrup, in that order. Look at the picture and see if you agree.

These three bones touch each other. One end of the malleus touches the anvil, but the other touches the tympanic membrane (the eardrum). When a sound wave vibrates the eardrum, the malleus moves back and forth, too. This starts the anvil moving. The anvil, in turn, moves the stapes because it touches it. The other end of the stapes is in contact with the liquid which fills the inner ear, through the tiny opening in the thin layer of bone between the middle and inner ear. The stapes fits tightly in place. No liquid moves backward into the middle ear. The

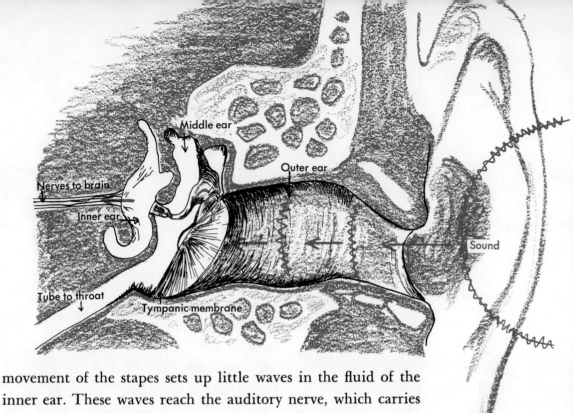

Middle ear

Outer ear

Nerves to brain

Inner ear

Sound

Tube to throat

Tympanic membrane

movement of the stapes sets up little waves in the fluid of the inner ear. These waves reach the auditory nerve, which carries the message to the brain.

These three little bones carry not only the sound waves, they also make them bigger, magnifying the waves at least ten times. The three ear bones act in series to increase the wave of sound which first reached the malleus through the tympanic membrane which separates the middle ear from the outside ear.

Sound waves can also reach the inside of the ear through the temporal bone, but the sound waves need to be much stronger to pass through bone than through the membrane and inner ear.

Whatever bones in your body you can feel, one thing is sure. You cannot see or feel the malleus, incus, or stapes. They are well protected in their little space within the temporal bone.

How Bones and Muscles
Work Together

You walk up and down stairs; reach down to pick up a ball and throw it; bite into an apple; roller-skate; run for a bus; write a letter. You can do all these things without any difficulty at all, without really thinking about it.

Yet all these motions are different. None would be possible without bones and the muscles which are attached to them.

All the bones together make up the skeleton of the human body. The muscles which are attached to them are called the skeletal muscles. There are other kinds of muscles, too, such as those over which one has no control, muscles of the heart, intestines and so on. However, it is the skeletal muscles which make it possible to walk, throw a ball and do all the thousand and one things which require motion.

Everyone is familiar with animal muscle; steaks, chops, lamb, and pork are all muscle of one or another animal. In the human, muscle makes up 40 percent of the weight of the body. Muscles are of many different sizes. There is a muscle in the middle ear which is only a very tiny fraction of an inch long. On

the other hand, the calf of the leg is almost entirely one big muscle.

Working with the muscles are the tendons. They join the muscles to bones. These are very strong, tough cords or ribbons of tissue. You can see them very well on the back of your hand, especially if your hand is thin. They run from the wrist to the end of the fingers. When you make a fist you can see them move. Also working with the bones, helping to hold them together at the joints, are other strong flexible bands called ligaments (lig'-ah-ments).

A joint is the place in the body where two bones come together. The shoulder, elbow, and wrist are examples of joints. There are, of course, others. The joints make motion possible.

Joints are of several kinds and serve many different purposes.

Bones of the arm with a large muscle contracted.

Tendons of the hand

A *hinge joint* works like the hinge of a door; movement is in only one direction. Can you give an example of a hinge joint? Stop to think a moment. Here are two examples: the ankle and the knee.

There are *ball and socket joints*. In such a joint one end of the bone can roll around in the hollowed-out space of the bone it fits into. A shoulder is such a joint. The head of the humerus in the arm is rounded and fits into the scapula, or shoulder bone. Move your shoulder. You can feel the ball and socket motion. You can move the shoulder in any direction.

A *saddle joint* allows even more freedom of motion. The base of the thumb is a good example. The free movement of the thumb has done a great deal to help man conquer the hostile world of nature. It has made it possible for the hand to grasp objects, and and by so doing man has been able to hold and use tools and weapons — to make and use large things and very small things. Sometime tie your thumb so it can't move. You will quickly find you can't do many things which you can usually do easily.

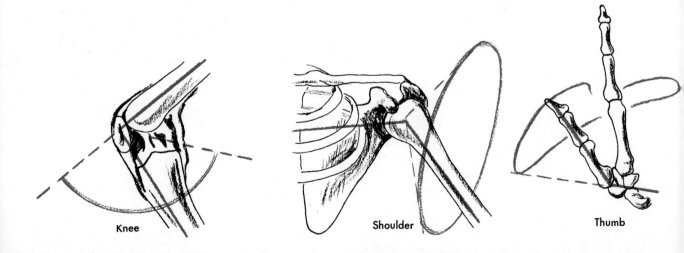

Knee   Shoulder   Thumb

Muscles usually work in pairs. When one shortens (contracts) to move a joint, another muscle has to lengthen to allow the movement. This is easily seen in moving the fingers to make a fist. Obviously the muscles which move the tendons on the inside of the fingers are now short, the muscles which move the tendons on the outside, long.

The action of muscles can also be seen in the upper arm. When the fist is clenched and the elbow bent, the muscles on the inside of the upper arm bulge. One of these is called the biceps muscle.

An amazingly large number of motions are made possible by the different ways the muscles and tendons move the bones. The bones are the necessary framework for muscular action.

47

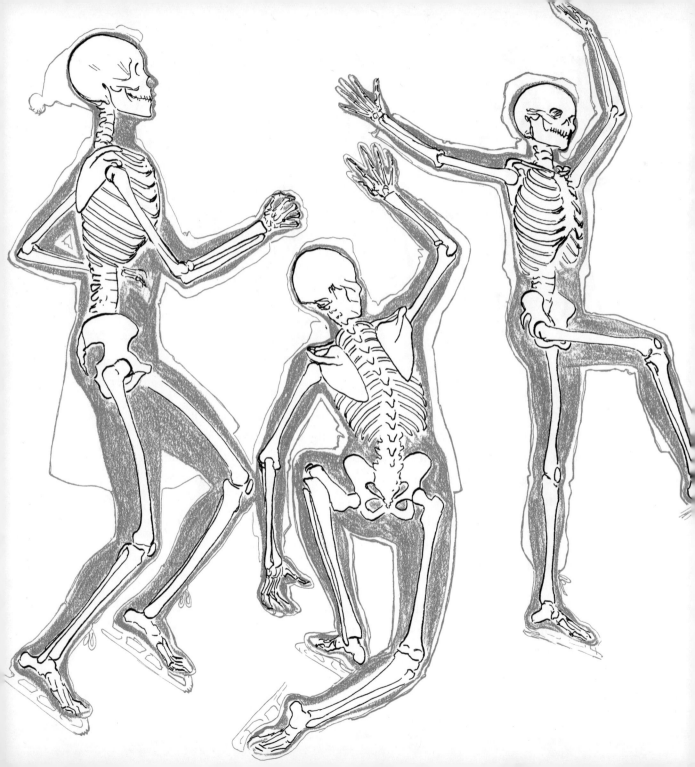

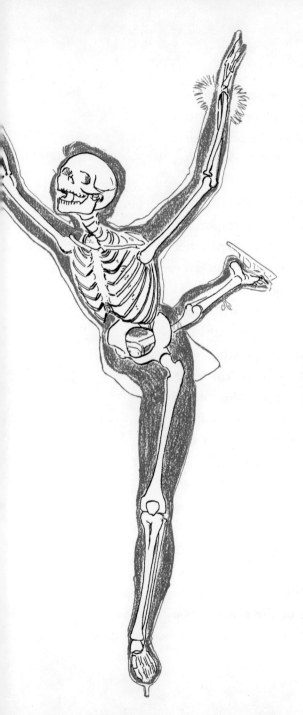

The pictures show some of these motions. You will certainly think of many more. Notice how the shape of the skeleton changes to suit the motion.

Although you run, jump, and take your bones and muscles through many different acts, you do this without thinking about what you are doing. You don't, for instance, tell each muscle just how it should move. Very few people — only experts — could even name all the muscles which are joined to bones. Actually you acquire this skill over a very long time, starting from the day you are born. A baby is about five months old before he is able to grasp a toy. He tries and fails and tries again. His brain sends orders through the nerves to the muscles, and when the muscles finally do what the brain tells them, a pattern is set up. Each time the infant grasps the toy his muscles are surer of the lesson learned. The same is true of every movement the body makes. When the pattern is well made, no time passes between the thought and the action, or at least the time is so short it can hardly be measured.

How the brain and nerves work is another story, told in another book. Everything about the way the body works is a wonderful tale.

49

Bones Protect the Body

An earlier chapter tells how the temporal bone of the skull protects the three tiny bones of hearing, as well as keeping safe other parts of the hearing apparatus. What other parts of the body do bones protect?

It is clear, once you think about it, that some parts of the body are more important than others. If you lost a toe it would not make a great difference to you. It would be worse to lose a foot or a hand. Life would certainly be much more difficult with only one arm instead of two, or one leg instead of two legs. Yet life would still be possible.

There are other parts of the body which are necessary for life, for example, the brain. Small injuries to the brain may not be fatal. It depends on where the damage is. In one place an injury may cause blindness, in another inability to speak. Any large damage, however, will bring death. Therefore the brain needs to be well protected, and it is. The bones which make up the skull are tightly fitted together. There is no space between them for even a thin knife to get in. Moreover, the very shape of the skull is one

50

which makes for the greatest protection. It is a dome, just about the strongest shape possible. It will withstand very heavy blows, especially blows from the top, which is the part most likely to be hit by falling objects. You already know how strong bone itself is. The shape of the skull is added protection to the brain within it.

The skull rests on the spine — the column of vertebrae. Each vertebra has a hole right through its center not unlike the hole in a doughnut. Through this hole runs the spinal cord. At the top, the spinal cord joins the brain. The spinal cord is a column of nerve tissue. From it nerves go out to other parts

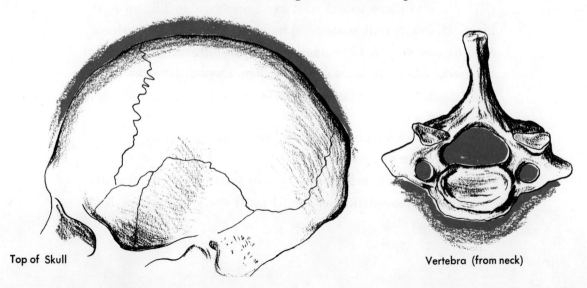

Top of Skull   Vertebra (from neck)

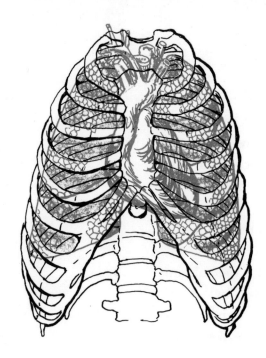

Bones make a strong cage around the heart and lungs

of the body. The spinal cord is almost as important to life as the brain is.

If the brain and spinal cord are important to life, so is the heart. It, too, is well guarded. The heavy sternum (breastbone) and the ribs attached to each side of it are joined to vertebrae at the back. All these make a strong cage around the heart. Muscles attached to the ribs, breastbone, and spine give additional protection.

The same cage which protects the heart also serves to shield the lungs from harm.

You can readily feel the sternum in your own body, feel how the cage of ribs extends backward until the ribs join the back-bone (spine).

This ends the story of living bone. Of course not everything about bones has been told in these few pages. Every day something new is being learned about them. There are experts who study bones and nothing else. Doctors who deal with the muscles, joints, and bones are called orthopedic (or-tho-peed'-ic) surgeons.

Dead bones, as well as living bones, have many interesting tales to tell. Most valuable, perhaps, are those about the development of man in the days of prehistory, the days before man learned to write. Prehistory lasted many tens of thousands of years. In Egypt writing dates back only 5,000 to 6,000 years. In the Americas prehistory is the time before the Spanish came. Indians had no written history. Let's look now at a few ways in which bone tells stories of ancient man.

charcoal from fire places
Bones
stone tools

A
B

stone tools   Bones
charcoal
C14 29500 ± 1500
Rocks fell from the
top of the cave

C

charcoal
fire places

D

flint tools
charcoal
Bones of a
child of about
nine years old

25 feet

54

The Stories Dead Bones Tell

A few years ago, in Brooklyn, N.Y., men remodeling an old house dug up some skeletons. What a to-do! Had murder been done here? Police came. The bones were carried away for experts to examine. The conclusion: the piece of land had probably been a cemetery. The bones might be a hundred years old, no more.

The Brooklyn discovery was of no great interest to scientists. They are most interested in bones thousands of years old, especially in bones of very early man which will show how man became man, learned to walk upright and to use his hands in making tools.

Almost halfway around the world from Brooklyn, and not too long ago, either, scientists were digging in a cave looking for traces of early man, man before he was civilized. It is seldom that bones of early man — or animals either — can be found. However, caves are good places in which to dig. Man could live in caves, protected from the rain, the wind, the sun. In caves man could be safe from wild animals. Lions can be dangerous today. You can imagine how frightening they were when man had no weapons but his hands, perhaps a stone, or later in history, spears.

The particular cave these scientists were exploring was Shanidar Cave in the Zagros Mountains in northern Iraq. They had outstanding luck. They dug through layer after layer of dirt, the accumulation of centuries. At levels of 14 to 23 feet below the surface they found human bones. It was estimated that one skeleton was 45,000 years old and another probably 60,000 years old.

Now that is certainly a very long time ago. It was a great many thousands of years before there was any written language. How, then, could these scientists tell how old the bones were?

They were able to do so because of the discovery of carbon-14 in 1946.

Of course you know what carbon is. It is one of the most important elements. Without carbon there would be no life. Every plant, every animal, contains carbon combined with many other elements. Every animal — including you! — breathes in the oxygen through its lungs. The blood carries the oxygen away from the lungs, the body cells use it, then combine it with waste carbon to make carbon dioxide, which the blood carries back to the lungs. Then it is breathed out again into the outside air. The plants then use it, give off oxygen, and the cycle starts over.

All this has been known for a long time. What was new was the discovery that the carbon in some carbon dioxide in the air was not just ordinary carbon but was radioactive.

There are a number of substances (such as those of the uranium type) which are not very stable. Their atoms change their structure, giving off "radiations." This activity is called radioactivity. It is not affected by anything outside the substance itself, but proceeds at a regular rate. The time required for a given amount of a radioactive substance to give off one-half its radiation is called its half-life. If you had a piece of radioactive substance which weighed a pound, and after one year there was only one-half a pound of the radioactive chemical present and the rest was the ordinary variety, then the half-life of that sub-

arbon C12 and   Radiocarbon C14

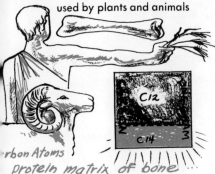

used by plants and animals

rbon Atoms

protein matrix of bone
gram of Carbonized bone
ives off indications of 15.3
disintegrations per minute

5,600 years pass

If they had a
geiger counter
they could read

7.65 disintegrations (clicks) per minute

half of the C-14 is
disintegrated

Another 5,600 years pass

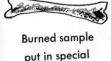

Burned sample
put in special
geiger counter

3.85 disintegrations (clicks) per minute

quarter of the original
C-14 remains

ould mean the bone died 11,200 years ago

stance would be one year. Each radioactive substance has its own half-life, some a millionth part of a second, others a million million years.

The half-life of carbon-14, it was found by experiments, was approximately 5,600 years. Scientists determined this by measuring its amount of radioactivity in comparison with that of other radioactive substances.

Now just what has this to do with the skeletons found in the cave in Iraq? How is carbon-14 useful in dating bones?

It works like this. As you have just read, everything that lives contains carbon. Plants get it by breathing in carbon dioxide. Animals get it by eating plants, or by eating animals which have eaten plants. Some, indeed most, of the carbon dioxide in the air is *not* radioactive, but some of it is carbon-14. It becomes radioactive by the action of cosmic rays in the atmosphere. This was true for millions of years before man even dreamed of an atom bomb.

Only one part in one million million parts of carbon dioxide is carbon-14, is radioactive. Now carbon-14 in the body gradually loses its radioactivity in the body, but as long as the body is living it takes on more carbon-14. After death, no more will be added to the amount in the body. The radioactivity gradually becomes less and less. In 5,600 years it will be just half what it was when the animal or plant died. In 11,200 years it will be one-half of one-half, or one-quarter, and so on. Thus by measuring the amount of carbon-14 in the bones found in caves and elsewhere, scientists can tell when the animal, including man, died.

Making these dating tests is not easy. There is radioactivity in the air all the time, and the radiation from bombs must be considered and screened out. So the tests have to be made in a large laboratory where all kinds of precautions are taken to get accurate results. Even so, no one claims the results are accurate to within a couple of hundred years.

Granting this, the dating is really quite good, and as more tests are made the results become more and more reliable. Radiocarbon dating has been a very great help in telling scientists dates of what happened long before written history. However, there is a limit to how far back in time the test can give even a relatively accurate date — probably no farther than 60,000 years.

It was this radiocarbon test which was used to date the Shanidar Cave skeletons.

Bones — of men or animals — are among the best objects for carbon-14 dating, for they are the only parts of the body which remain whole after thousands and thousands of years. Even if bones are broken, they can be tested. The bone does not have to be destroyed in order to make the test. Naturally scientists are most anxious that a rare bone should be left unharmed. There is only one other material which is likely to remain unchanged as long as bones; that is charcoal from fires. Charcoal is very good for carbon-14 dating, for it is practically pure carbon.

There is another method of dating bones which has been useful, especially before radioactive dating was available. This is fluorine dating. Water in certain soils contains the element fluorine combined in different forms. If a bone was found in such a soil, and water had flowed around it, the bone would contain fluorine. The amount of fluorine gives the approximate age of the bone. This test was very useful in exposing a famous fraud.

In 1908 part of skull was dug up in Piltdown, England. A few years later more of it was found near the same place. It became known as Piltdown man. The importance placed on the skull was very great, for it didn't fit into the usual picture of the history of the development of man, as shown by other skulls which had been found. The Piltdown skull led to a whole new line of thought. Scientists had many theories about it.

In 1948 a very small piece of bone from the skull was analyzed by chemical means. It was found that the fluorine content was only 0.2 percent. This put the skull in the same class as recent man — that is, only a few thousand years old, not hundreds of thousands.

Further examination showed that the lower jaw was not even that of a man, ancient or modern, but of a modern ape!

It was all a fraud. The bones had been treated to look old, and the teeth had actually been painted.

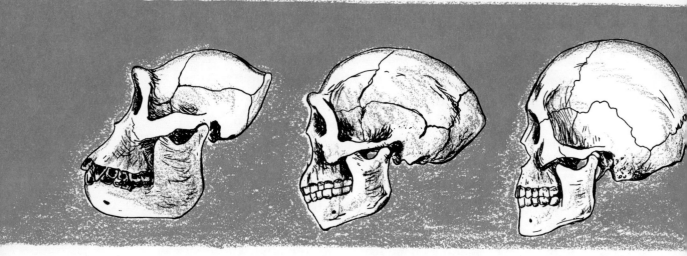

Ape   Early man   Modern man

Later, radiocarbon dating confirmed the date given by fluorine testing.

Dead bones still can tell us stories about early man before he learned to write, before he had learned to use any tools except the simplest ones made of stone.

And, just as the size of your bones tell your age, and the shape of certain bones can tell whether you are a boy or a girl, so the size and shape of ancient bones found in caves or in a few other places in the world, tell whether the bones were part of a man or a woman, an infant, or a boy or girl. Moreover, from the way the bone is broken, if it is broken, a good guess can be made that the man (or woman or child) was killed, or perhaps murdered.

In its own way, dead bone is as interesting as bone still alive. Do you agree?

60

GLOSSARY

artery — large blood vessel which carries blood from the heart

callus — a substance which bridges the gap between parts of a broken bone

cancellous — a kind of bony tissue which is spongy

capillary — a very tiny blood vessel which joins a small artery to a small vein

carbon-14 — a form of carbon which is radioactive

eardrum — see tympanic membrane

epiphysis — the end of a bone which is separate from it while the bone is still growing, after which it becomes part of the bone

fontanel — the open space between the bones of the skull of an infant

greenstick fracture — a bone which is bent not broken

half-life — the amount of time it takes a radioactive substance to lose half of its radioactivity

hemoglobin — the red substance of the red blood cell which carries oxygen from the lungs to the cells of the body

marrow — a soft substance which fills the cavities of most bones

matrix — the mesh or lattice-like part of bone, made up of a protein-like material

osseous tissue — bony tissue

periosteum — the covering of a bone

radioactive substance — one which is unstable, changing at a regular rate into a different material, giving off "radiations" as it does so

skeleton — all the bones of the body

spinal cord — a column of nerve tissue inside the backbone

tympanic membrane — the eardrum; the membrane which separates the outer ear from the middle ear

vein — large blood vessel which carries blood from the body back to the heart

Index

THE AUTHOR

Edith Weart majored in chemistry at Oberlin College and was a chemist at Mt. Sinai Hospital in Cleveland, Ohio. She has written many articles on medical subjects for the general reader. The author believes that young readers can understand and enjoy learning about the complex and fascinating mechanism that is the human body.

Miss Weart lives in Jackson Heights, New York.

THE ARTIST

The outstanding illustrations are by Jan Fairservis of Seattle, Washington, who has also illustrated two previous books in this series, THE STORY OF YOUR GLANDS and THE STORY OF YOUR RESPIRATORY SYSTEM.